HAS

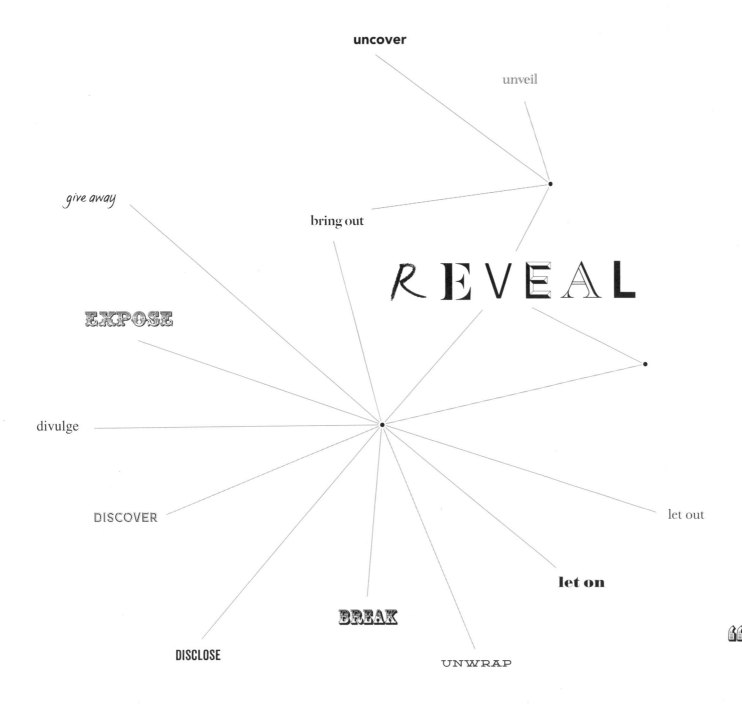

uncover

unveil

give away

bring out

REVEAL

EXPOSE

divulge

DISCOVER

let out

let on

BREAK

DISCLOSE

UNWRAP

Every man's work, whether it be literature or music or pictures or architecture or anything else, is always a portrait of himself."

Samuel Butler
The Way of All Flesh

DEDICATION

For my Pa who always showed me great love & kindness, & whom I miss daily.

REVEAL

INTERIOR DESIGN AS A REFLECTION OF WHO WE ARE

BY HARRIET ANSTRUTHER

CLEARVIEW

Published in the UK in 2014 by Clearview Books
25 Eccleston Place, London SW1W 9NF

A CIP record for this book is available from the British Library.
ISBN 978-1908337 221
Printed in China

Cover and Book design: Glad Creative
Production: Simonne Waud
Editor: Catharine Snow

REVEAL

**INTERIOR DESIGN
AS A REFLECTION
OF WHO WE ARE**

—

BY HARRIET
ANSTRUTHER

CLEARVIEW

Harriet

FOREWORD

BY TOM DIXON

An avalanche of influences and references, an explosion of
textures and a kaleidoscope of pattern. Rough worm-holed
sixteenth century beams or synthetic fluorescent laminates
jostle for attention with rude words and pop art prints - there
is no logical reason why this multitude of sensory stimulus
should work, but in the skilled hands of Harriet Anstruther,
a pattern is brought to the chaos, an hospitable order to the
contradictions, a generosity to the proceedings to create
a series of unexpected spaces for serious entertaining,
stimulating working or superior everyday living.

INTRODUCTION

'THIS BOOK ISN'T GOING
TO TEACH YOU ANYTHING.'

It won't seek to limit your creativity or imagination
with clever little design tips or hints on what is 'right'
or 'wrong'. It's not a tedious bible of rules, in which
generic formulae are didactically laid down, serving
only to smother your design sensibility. My motivation
springs from pure egotism; I only want to introduce you
to some of my work and a few of the things that have
inspired me, in the hope that they'll inspire you too.

What interests me is how design, particularly interior design,
allows us to examine our environment and ourselves. The
process can be a journey to reveal the core within. The images
shown in the book are therefore used as a narrative device
to show how and why I piece together a design puzzle, what
that says about me and the clients I work with, and why,
in some cases, people choose to reveal nothing at all.

My friends, family and colleagues will no doubt tell
you what an appallingly opinionated pain in the ass I
am; what an obsessive eye for detail I have, and that
I enjoy swearing and smoking far too much. These
foibles, and many more, will come to light on closer
inspection of this book, which after all, aims to shine
a more psychological light on the design process.

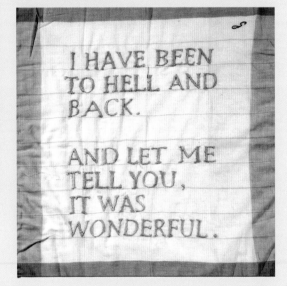

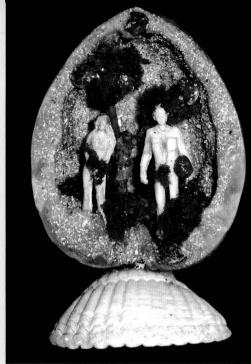

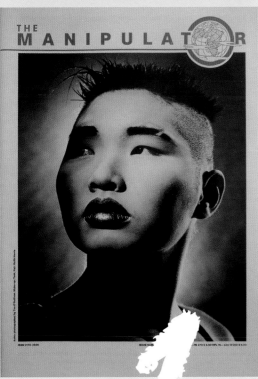

ROOTS /
THE ONEIRIC HOME

Our roots are the basic cause, the source, indeed the origin of our lives. They anchor us through memories or oneiric dream-memories that are often hard to shake off or break away from. If we like them, we need to replicate them to align us to whom we perhaps understand, desire or remember being; if we associate them with anxiety or maybe sadness, we will wish to ignore or even avoid them. So if, as Alain de Botton describes, the home is able to be a 'guardian of identity', should the interiors we have any control over, embody our personalities & can we chose how much they reveal about ourselves?

The French philosopher Gaston Bachelard wrote beautifully about the historical & emotional ties and attachments we may have to a former place or thing in his seminal book 'The Poetics of Space'. Consciously and unconsciously we revert to what we know and perhaps treasure or even loathe, when making decisions about what we chose to surround ourselves with. Keeping or reproducing versions of spaces or things we love for example, would seem to have therapeutic value as objects or rooms become versions of the things we found fascinating, happy or inspiring. This being said, the design of an interior space therefore has the potential and capacity to alter the way we can feel, function, think, relax, succeed, purchase, study, live or even die.

Interiors can also reflect religious beliefs or cultural references. Late Islamic design conscientiously omits any representation of the figurative, whilst the Shaker interior symbolises their strict, communal and monastic teachings. In both these examples, we see people in an acknowledged understanding of what visual things reveal about their owners.

☞ I spent much of my childhood in the countryside, watching
& listening to nature's rhythms. There are no straight lines in
nature; the curves & irregularities of the natural world, remind
us of ourselves, our frailties & strengths. The inevitable decay
& death of life around us, as wondrous as the gravity defying
bulbs that herald the return of Spring.

☞ "And though home is a
name, a word, it is a strong
one; stronger than magician
ever spoke, or spirit answered
to, in strongest conjuration."

Charles Dickens
Martin Chuzzlewit

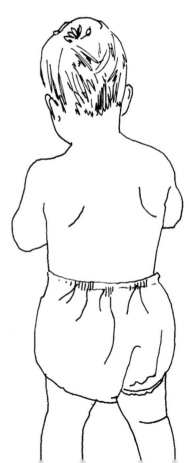

☞ "I am not what I am, I am
what I do with my hands…"

Louise Bourgeois

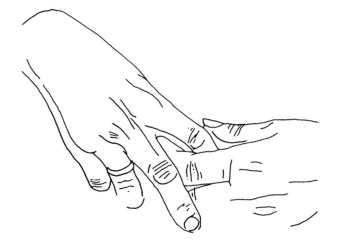

A NEED TO DISAPPEAR

Gaston Bachelard's influential book *The Poetics of Space* focuses especially on the "eulogised space". He states, "There is ground for taking the house as a tool for analysis of the human soul", describing the corner as "the germ of the room, or of a house". Indeed he devotes a chapter to corners, comparing them with shells and nests, claiming that "a corner that is 'lived in' tends to reject and restrain, even to hide life".

Francesca Woodman's work seems to embody this idea, working often in decrepit interiors, where the body becomes the space, and of people becoming the wall under the wallpaper, or of an extension of the wall onto floor.

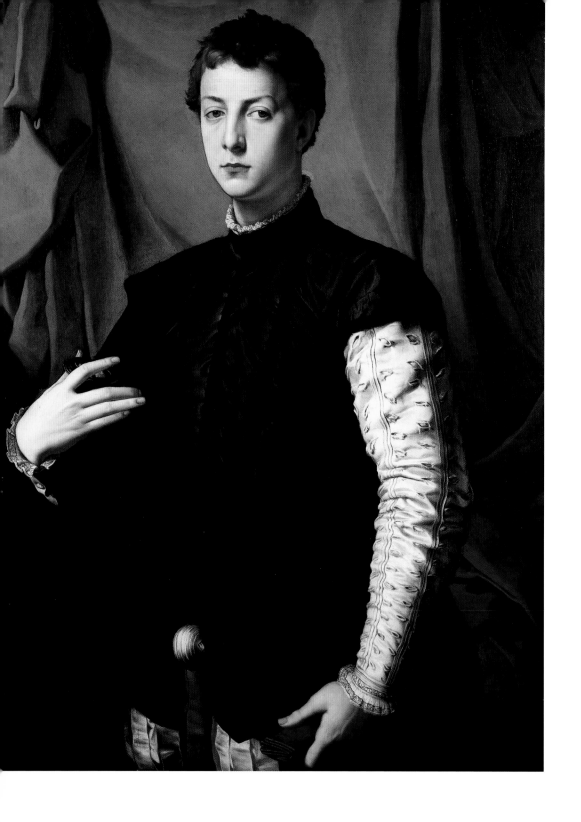

☛ RECREATING ASPECTS OF MEMORY.

The drawing room was a place we were strongly discouraged to enter unaccompanied as children. The scull cushions act as reminders of this warning as does the clock face with missing hands, indicating precious & irregular visits to a grown up world of treasures.

☞ SMALL THINGS

On the occasions my father came to town, he was often found at his writing bureau making lists. The many drawers within reflected his devotion to being 'ever-ready'; fuses, paper clips, pencils, miniature tools.

The art-piece hung above by Su Blackwell, beautifully captures his love of books and nature.

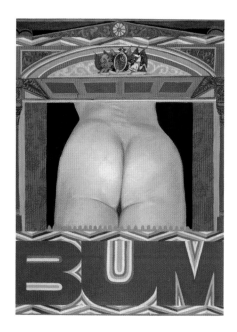

COLOUR MEETS DESIRE

Much of my early childhood
was spent at Ken & Kathleen
Tynan's house, with their
children Roxana & Matthew.
This painting by Pauline Boty
hung in the red dining room
between two large windows
to the street. It is a portrait
of Kathleen's beautiful bum.
I was radicalised early on.

JUXTAPOSITION
& STRUCTURE

If as John Donne famously penned "No man is an island entire of itself", can separate elements within an interior space visually exist alone? An interior may well be designed as an empty oasis of calm or perhaps a collector's home of themed paradisiacal luxury, but everything within it, relates in some way to its neighbour with contrasting or harmonious effect. Even an empty room houses varieties of textures, smells, tones, structures that cannot be read independently without producing combinations and connections that form the whole. Each detail therefore, each wall, light, picture, piece of furniture, book on a shelf, inevitably connects and contrasts with another thing, with our view of it, which creates an overall impression of a space.

Juhani Pallasmaa wrote a book that inspired me greatly, called 'The Eyes of the Skin'. In it he discusses this theme amongst others, noting that interiors and architecture can lend themselves to spiritual essence, rather than isolated retinal pictures. Since interiors are created around their inhabitants, whether an elephant enclosure, or a home for humans, the scale is necessarily taken into account and the fact that the physical forms inside the space are merely objects among other objects.

I vacillate endlessly between desiring sparseness on the one hand, and personal paraphernalia on the other. So I move things about to create connections, arranging and re-arranging, whilst recalling the modernist Eugenia Errazuriz's stubborn insistence that "A house that doesn't alter is a dead house". For an Edwardian, her views on anti-clutter were unheard of, but over a lifetime, as our moods change, why shouldn't our surroundings to suit them?

A BEDROOM FOR DREAMING

"Upon the purple tree-tops far away, and on the green height near at hand up which the shades were slowly creeping, there was an equal hush. Between the real landscape and its shadow in the water, there was no division; both were so untroubled and clear, and, while so fraught with solemn mystery of life and death, so hopefully reassuring to the gazer's soothed heart, because so tenderly and mercifully beautiful."

Charles Dickens
Little Dorrit

STRUCTURE LAID BARE

Rafters appear as ribs in which we, the inhabitants, act as the beating heart of the room. The tie beams, posts, purlins & the like, were often made from pre-used timbers bearing boat-maker's markings.

can·ti·le·ver
[kan-tl-ee-ver, -ev-er]
noun
1.
any rigid structural member
projecting from a vertical
support, especially one in
which the projection is great
in relation to the depth,
so that the upper part is in
tension and the lower part
in compression.

☞ SIDE BY SIDE

By placing furniture in
a particular way, we are
creating a delicate system
of signs as a means to
communicate; the angle
of the chairs in strict straight
lines, or human curves
around a focal point.

GROUPIE

Lucy Rie ceramics set out
below a Henry Bourne
photograph of a sleep-
measuring machine.

☞ A Caragh Thuring painting
takes centre stage above an
amalgam of objects in black
& white.

49

☞ "I have ideas in my head only because I have images." **Voltaire**

Since I collect like a magpie, I tend to place pictures on ledges, shelves, sills, mantles etc… so that they can be moved about and edited with ease.

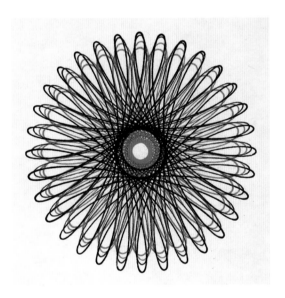

CURVACEOUS

When the Romans invented architectural arches, they were naturally thought of as an accomplishment & thereafter used as symbols of triumph. I enjoy the contrast of curves, arches, circle's with linear vertical & horizontal lines. They feed off each other, altering straightforward structure with whimsy.

SHELTER

We all need shelter; somewhere at its most basic, that provides us with water, light & heat. At best, our own shelter or home gives us among other things, sanctuary, protection, safety and intimacy, and cradles us like a man-made shell. Our homes are also of course our kingdoms, our castles, giving us reassurance & privacy, & a place to display our life trophies.

My two favourite places of shelter & retreat are my bedroom and my garden shed. I especially love to sit in the latter when it is raining outside; the windier & wetter, the better to feel secluded, shielded, apart. The word shed is etymologically related to the word 'shade' or 'a dark dwelling'. This of course conjures up secret dens, where as children my siblings & I created worlds within worlds that we could control ourselves whilst providing us with space to imagine & withdraw. One of our first dens was on a steep woodland bank, under the roots of a large, old beech tree. I remember finding some blue & white checked linoleum tiles in the rubbish one day & taking them up to our nest to create shelves for a pink plastic tea set. I would sweep out our earthy home & endlessly play house, building bonfires to cook experimental picnics.

Since one of my favourite pleasures is reading, my bed provides me with the ultimate sheltered solitude & the comfort I crave. I was interested to discover that even the Romans had small, private chambers for sleeping or reading, known as 'cubiculum', which is where the word cubicle is derived from. The Medieval four-poster was designed not just for grandeur & statement, but also for privacy and protection from drafts, since dwellings were largely single rooms or halls without partitions. By the 17th century, a Parlor (from the French word 'parlez') and later a Withdrawing Chamber, now known as a Drawing Room, were in use for increased privacy, after which, from the early 1800s, the Victorians went mad. Separate ritual spaces were in vogue for smoking, sewing, eating, reading, talking etc. Each one had its strictly defined purpose which was radically different from the medieval and now equally modern desire for open-plan living.

☞ "PHILIP JOHNSON IS A HIGHBROW.

A highbrow is a man educated beyond his
capacity. His house is a box of glass – not
shelter. The meaning of the word shelter
includes privacy."

Frank Lloyd Wright

INNER SANCTUM

We are possibly at our most vulnerable whilst sleeping. Soothe yourself into a place of safety & dream state, with associations of childhood fantasy and play.

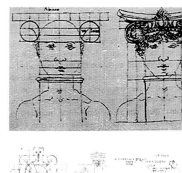

☞ 'I shambled after as usual
as I've been doing all my life
after people that interest me,
because the only people
that interest me are the mad
ones, the ones who are mad
to live, mad to talk, desirous
of everything at the same
time, the ones that never
yearn or say a commonplace
thing... but burn, burn, burn
like roman candles across
the night.'

Jack Kerouac
On The Road

☛ "I believe in plenty of optimism and white paint."

Elsie de Wolfe

FIRE & RAIN

Our basic human need for heat and water makes the kitchen the centre of a house from which most other necessities radiate.

No longer counted as merely a room to prepare & eat meals in, it is invariably where children sit to do their homework & families congregate after a busy day.

 The placing of candles or children's shoes in nooks within a home was thought, in medieval times, to shelter the house from the devil.

The colour blue is thought beneficial to the mind and body. It slows human metabolism whilst producing a calming effect to aid rest.

☞ ALL THAT GLITTERS

The client wanted a dark sitting room to withdraw to quietly at night. She also wanted it to act as a party room that could appear both traditional & secretly eccentric. Walls were painted with black and silver glitter paint that sparkled when hit with light.

SHIELD ME

The bathroom as a refuge
& retreat; it is thought that
the word shelter may derive
from the 15th century word
meaning 'locked shields',
providing cover, protection
& refuge.

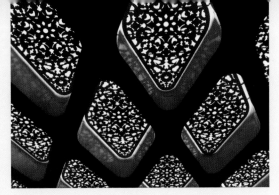

LIGHT & SHADOW

Light is a source of wellbeing, and is widely used as therapy by medical & spiritual practitioners the world over. In Ayurvedic medicine, the use of coloured light is also thought to correct imbalances in the body. What better way then to begin the morning, under a magenta pink skylight that not only disguises winter white skin, but literally starts your day as though through rose-tinted glasses. Skylights or indeed glass floors allow us to see spaces through spaces, vistas of structure & life taking place elsewhere, whilst we stand still.

Most people want the spaces they live & work in to be well lit & bright but the darkness & the shadows can be welcome too. Living in England means long, dark usually wet winters, a time when we crave sunlight & warmth, but there is also something gratifyingly restful after a long day, unwinding in an ambient dimly lit room, where candles cast shadows.

Both dazzling light & dim light allow us to see our surroundings in silhouette. The shapes created add drama and definition and a further dimension to familiar contexts. Perhaps the best example of this is a country walk in the moonlight, when everything seems magically transformed & clear, the shapes as interesting & sometimes abstract as the objects themselves. I'm a big fan of the photographer Susan Derges, whose cameraless photographs of nature capture the essence and unreality of moonlight. When she first began her career as an abstract painter, she explained that, "it offered the promise of being able to speak of the invisible rather than to record the visible". Her photographs manage to do this too.

Last year I travelled to Japan for the first time. In Kyoto, I was entranced by the vivid clarity of the daylight that made some species of trees in particular, look like reflections. Pools of water became mirrors & colours appeared different from any I had seen before. It left me feeling uplifted and light headed.

entrance 1 *(ˈɛntrəəns)*
— n
1. the act or an instance
of entering; entry

2. a place for entering,
such as a door or gate

3a. the power, liberty, or
right of entering; admission
3b. (as modifier): an
entrance fee

4. the coming of an actor or
other performer onto a stage
[C16: from French,
from entrer to enter]

entrance 2 *(ˈɛntrəəns)*
— vb
1. to fill with wonder
and delight; enchant
2. to put into a trance;
hypnotize

☞ NATURE VS NURTURE

Natural daylight emits a very particular mood to a room that changes during the hours of the day & seasons of the year. Its softness is dreamy & romantic.

BRINGING THE OUTSIDE IN

Henry Bourne's exceptional
Folklore series, evoking rural
pastimes in a modern setting.

☞ ILLUSIONS

It is fun to use natural &
man-made light to expose
or hide, bring out & unveil,
or glimpse to discover
something bit by bit.

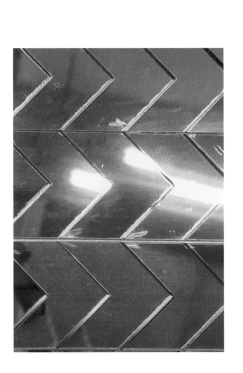

☞ NORTHERN LIGHT

Artists have longed used
north light, also known as
reflected light, to get greater
control over contrasts and
subtle changes in tone
& colour. It produces a
coolness in rooms, a soft
light without the stark
variations of bright south
facing light. Rooms facing
north therefore, appear
different in colour even
if painted the same as
their counterparts.

☞ SILHOUETTE

Objects in a space alter in stark light, revealing their shape, contour & form.

At art school we had to spend many hours painting things in black & white tones only, which proved useful practice in developing an eye for tonal change & outline.

☞ REFLECTION

Most evenings I kick back
listening to rhythm & blues
music. I have had a lifetime's
obsession for Jimi Hendrix,
in particular his instrumental
version of the song 'Bold as
Love'. Turn up the volume.

"The reflection of the world
is blues, that's where that
part of the music is at. Then
you got this other kind of
music that's tryin' to come
around."

Jimi Hendrix

MATERIALITY
& COLOUR

Inevitably we use all our senses when entering a space. Some people are more in tune with these than others, and some choose positively to ignore them. The haptic or non-verbal responses we get from the scent, colours, textures, sounds of a space help us understand elements of its function & are keys to who inhabitants it. By sending us signals with which to understand better our surroundings, these subtle sensations give us what we call the feel or mood of a place. Gaston Bachelard referred to them as "bearing the essence of a home".

Since we are all very different, what I might find uplifting, you may find depressing, so creating a mood that multiple people like, is not altogether straightforward. Many years ago, I was very generously lent a small house to live in with my daughter who at the time was four. It was at a difficult period & I was most grateful for the loan, however it was a place that never felt right. No matter what I did to it, I simply could not alter the negative vibe of the house. I tried re-arranging the furniture, painting it, moving things about to no avail. We were not happy there & the house was not happy to have us. My eyes liked it, but my skin didn't.

In order to produce successful work, creative people must tap into their sixth, more 'heightened' sense. As discussed in Chapter 1, I often find myself reverting to my roots & memories unconsciously when designing; an apple green that reminds me of my mother's 2CV, a neon pink velvet that matches a pair of trousers my rather shy father used to wear in the evening, and an unnatural dislike of yellow as it reminds me of a dress my grandmother had made me that itched like crazy.

To realize the idea of a heightened sense, I mix up textures and objects with gay abandon. I use this juxtapositioning to soften, glamourize, inject, cleanse and stimulate. I'm attracted to the process of it collecting our data and changing over time; the home as a historic timepiece, soaking up atmospheres and our DNA.

'The hands want to see, the eyes want to caress'
Goethe

COLOUR-ME-TASTIC

I can only assume that my love of certain pink shades comes from the lack of them in my childhood wardrobe. As the middle child of five, most of my clothes were hand-me-downs & it was therefore a rarity to have something bought especially. My mother tells me I had a very keen eye for colour & texture from an early age, & on the occasions I was able to choose something, I was invariably drawn to pink.

THE ROUGH & THE SMOOTH

Whilst working for Yohji Yamamoto in 2012, I visited Nishiki food market in Kyoto, Japan. The colours & textures stunned me & I decided to adapt them into a rural interior I was doing in England. The room (right) was designed as a modern, residential schoolroom where the client's small children could be home educated. I wanted to combine rough & smooth textures with bright colours and gunmetal grey, to fire the imagination & get the senses sprung. Yves Klein's work (below) did just this for me when I was first shown it.

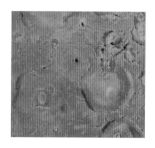

I have long been obsessed with black & white; a check, a stripe, a dot. The clarity of the combination gives me a sensation of both glamour & functionality. Since little in life is ever black or white, its presence brings me both calm and energy.

HAND MADE

The bespoke Tracey Boyd skull cushion & the Howe Greyhound settee, both bear their craftsmanship proudly. Seeing the hand-made quality of things gives them extra resonance and an opportunity to understand their textural layers.

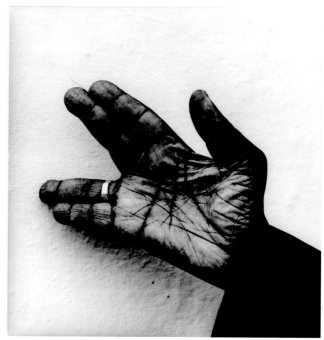

LAYERS OF LIFE

It's impossible to throw out
this chair, despite the insides
falling out. The guts reveal
its construction and current
use; wool, leather, metal,
cotton, woven coconut
fibres, horsehair, dog-hair.

Yayoi Kusama & the astonishing Louise Bourgeois. These women have both dealt with what life has thrown at them through their art. I am drawn to the heartbreak and bravery of their work, the rawness & the honesty.

"There is something very special in being able to sublimate your unconscious, and something very painful in the access to it…"

Louise Bourgeois

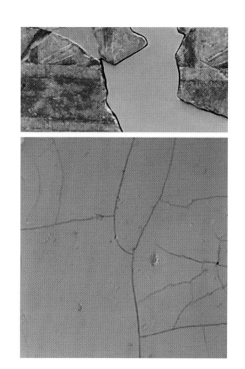

HEAD GIRL

Twatt →

TREASURES & CORBUSIER'S 'ROMANTIC COBWEBS'

One of my all-time favourite books is Signs of the Times by Nicholas Barker with photographs by Martin Parr. It captures beautifully the human psyche in terms of the relationships we have with our homes and the things we choose to put in them. All those incidental treasures we pick have become powerful shortcuts to memories, bringing therapeutic value and sustenance to a range of emotions.

William Morris & his Arts & Crafts Movement in the late 19th century were astringently against keeping anything that served no useful purpose. In the early 1930's, the Modernist Movement once again rallied against extraneous decoration, with Corbusier deridingly referring to any un-functional clutter as 'romantic cobwebs'. I would argue however, that the treasures we all keep, collect, perhaps unreasonably cherish, and often display, are what make the spaces we live in our own. These 'cobwebs' may have no meaning or function except the positive reactions they emit, that as humans we need. Subjected to Corbusier's functions of a house, rooms become merely cells in which to work, cook or rest, surely undermining nature, indeed opposing her. Our natures may be tamable but who wants to live like an automaton, beheading the hope or nourishment of beauty? Interestingly, Morris thought that if objects were considered beautiful, then the anti-clutter rule could be waived & Stendhal thought that indeed '…beauty was a promise of happiness' but that '…there are many styles of beauty as there are visions of happiness'.

One of my visions of happiness are casts or images of hands. Human hands symbolise both actions & meaning. A caress, a warning, a hit, a nurturing hand, a protective hand, something that is hand-made.

When I think of the people I know well, I visualise their hands as much as their faces; my mother picking red-currents over a weekend, which despite loathing to eat, made a marvelous pink colour when mixed (and left uneaten), with yoghurt. During the week, I would walk home from primary school to her architectural practice, to find her sitting on a dark red leather stool at her drawing board with a Rotary pen in hand & ink stains on her fingers. Often the red of the current juice still staining them, mixed with the black pen ink, made a deep dark purple dye, which appeared variously on her paperwork.

My father's hands were quite different. He lived quietly in the country, writing his books and walking, walking. I missed him dreadfully during the week and would run in to see him on a Friday night for a hug on arrival in Sussex. He was invariably sitting in his armchair by the fire with a book and a large Martini. On greeting, he would raise both hands from his lap in a small flutter, squeezing his eyes shut and smiling and say "Oh Hats". His hands had a distinct curve from thumb-tip to knuckle. I picture him shaking out his linen napkin before a meal, threading new laces on his boots, holding his walking stick & of course writing.

I group my treasures sometimes via a common theme or themes & at times based on silhouette or colour or height. The order brings me clarity, inspiration, calmness. What appears to be a random arrangement to others, acts as an intimate museum of items, which reveal a bit of who I am, and who my family are. Make of them what you will.

☞ PLEASURE

It's ridiculous what pleasure
some effects bring.

Henry Miller described that
a good feeling *"....put velvet
between vertebrae"* in his
book Tropic of Cancer.

I am drawn to words & their
myriad meanings in differing
contexts.

Might the reel of tickets be
a rule in life?

Life, ———

I am of both of your directions

Some how remaining hanging downward
the most

but strong as a cobweb in the
wind - I exist more with the glistening frost.
my beaded rays have colors I've
seen in a painting - ah life they
have cheated you

trompe l'oeil [*French* trawnp **lœ**-yuh; *English* **trawmp ley, loi**] -n

1. visual deception, especially in paintings, in which objects are rendered in extremely fine detailemphasizing the illusion of tactile and spatial qualities.

2. a painting, mural, or panel of wallpaper designed to create such an effect.

Origin:
1895–1900; < French: literally, (it) fools the eye

☞ I like to draw. I like to lie down. I like to read.

👆 "I remember Francis Bacon would say that he felt he was giving art what he thought it previously lacked. With me, it's what Yeats called the fascination with what's difficult. I'm only trying to do what I can't do."

Lucian Freud

TICKETS ON A LOOP

Beautiful, practical, useless

☞ LIFE AS A LOTTERY

Osita Nwankwo's striking
painting entitled A Man &
A Woman

1930's teaching cards hung around a house, provide reminders of what were deemed important actions & aspirations for children & adults alike. They still pack a punch.

SAVOR KINDNESS BECAUSE CRUELTY IS ALWAYS POSSIBLE LATER

☛ When I was small, our large tomcat Jerry gifted me one morning with a dying bird. Woken from a slumber, Jerry gently lowered the bird onto my pillow. It was a tiny Willow Tit whose heart I felt beating and then stop.

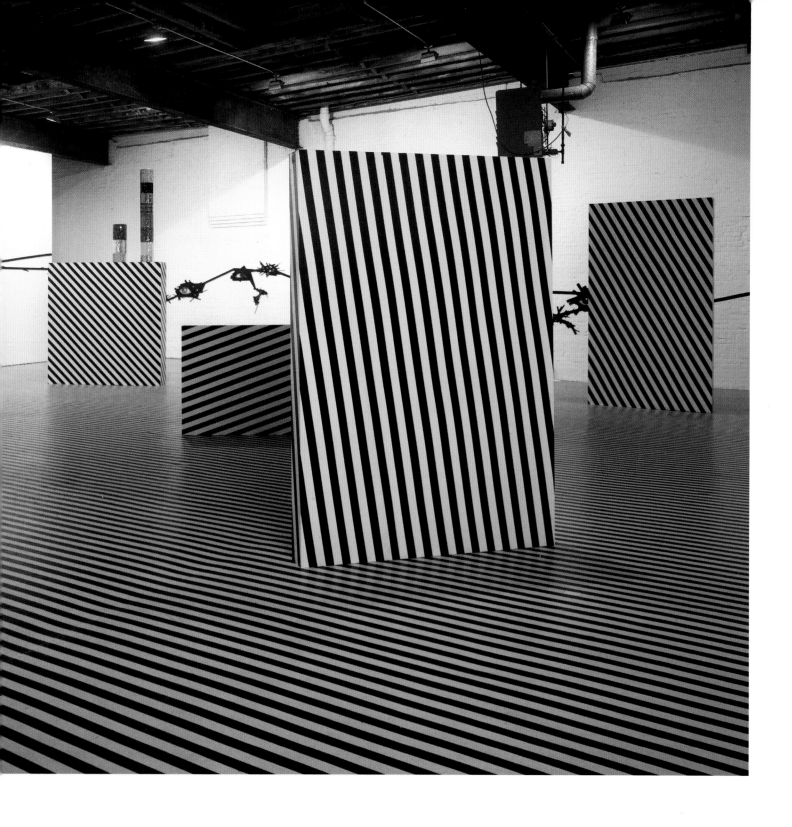

FEELING & GOOD
JUDGMENT

"If there is a reason for
keeping the wall very quiet,
choose a pattern that works
all over without pronounced
lines... Put very succinctly,
architectural effect depends
upon a nice balance of
horizontal, vertical and
oblique. No rules can say
how much of each; so
nothing can really take
the place of feeling and
good judgment."

William Morris

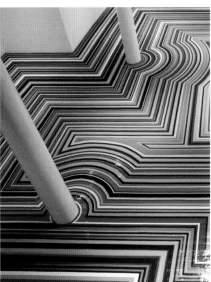

An inspirational Anni Albers drawing
& Jim Lambie having fun.

David Bowie. Enough said.

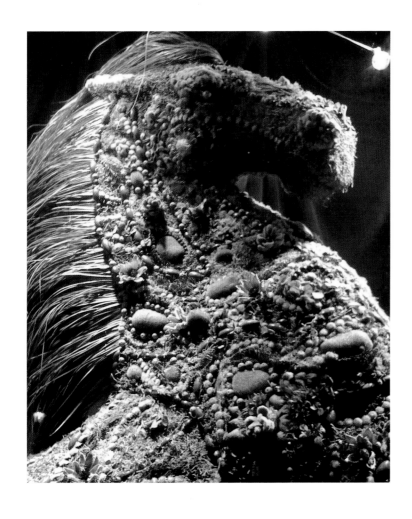

☛ BEATING HEART

I was raised to question, challenge, observe. We were encouraged to look & touch. I grew up in London with moulded plastic furniture, type-writers, pictures, antique chairs, hessian wallpaper; I grew up in Sussex with books, hedgerows, meadows, animals, straw bales, bones. My family are eccentric.

PLEASE GO SL
THE

OWLY ROUND
BEND

ARTISTS

Anni Albers
p147 (top right): *Drawing for a Rug*, © the Josef and Anni Albers Foundation

Celestia Anstruther
p16 (second from right): *Mona Lisa*
p115: *After Egon Schiele, 2011*

Harriet Anstruther
p16 (bottom): *Illustration of small boy on the beach*
p18 (bottom): *Pen and ink illustration of hands*
p133: *Illustration of Celestia resting*

David Austen
p12 (third column, bottom): *The Couple by David Austen courtesy of the Ingleby Gallery*
p24 (right): *Smoke Town, 2009*

James Basire
p76 (right): *Etching of Scottish woman in tartan shawl*

Pauline Boty
p31 (left): *Bum. Commissioned by Kenneth Tynan 1966, courtesy of the Pauline Boty Estate/Whitford Fine Art*

Francois Boucher
p16 (second from left): *Putti with birds by Francois Boucher, 1730*

Louise Bourgeois
p12 (second column, bottom): *"I've been to hell….". Textile, 1996, reproduced courtesy of the Louise Bourgeois Foundation.*

Henry Bourne
p15 (left): *Rose still life*
p15 (right): *Dead snipe still life*
p48 (right): *Sleep Machine*
p92: *Folklore Series*
p79: *Photography montage of water*
p100: *Insect Still Life*

Ruth Bricklan
p12 (fourth column, top): *Adam & Eve Walnut by Ruth Brickland, Reproduced courtesy of Ruth Bricklan*

Bronzino
p24 (left): *Painting of Lodovico Capponi by Bronzino, c.1550-1555, Frick Museum Collection, New York*

Patrick Caulfield
p131: *Trompe L'Oeil study on the artist studio door*

Susan Derges/ Ingleby Gallery
p83 (left): *Starfield Thistle photograph*

Tomas Downes
p113 (left): *Untitled, 2011*

Richard Gasper
p95 (left): *Untitled 2012*

Francesco di Giorgio
p62 (top right): *Origin of the capital of an Ionic column From the Magliabecchiano Codex, folio 33v*

Barry Kamen
p117 (middle top): *Drawing of hand in ink with paint coloured circles, on printed text, 1999*

Yves Klein
p110 (right): *Moon RP21 1960, reproduced courtesy of the Yves Klein Foundation*

Jim Lambie
p146: *Jim Lambie Brick House, reproduced courtesy of The Modern Institute, Glasgow*
p147 (right): *Art installation. Coloured flooring, reproduced courtesy of The Modern Institute, Glasgow*

Harland Miller
p30: *Incurable Romantic Seeks Dirty Filthy Whore, 2004*

Joan Miro
p80 (second from left, bottom): *Pitchfork, Foundation Maeght, 2012*

Michael Moebius
p130 (left): *Marilyn Bubble Gum, 2013*

Osita Nwankwo
p141: *A Man and A Woman, 2012*

Bruce Rae
p30 (centre on mantle-piece): *Small Bird, 2010*

Raphael
p16 (top right): *Tempi Madonna by Raphael circa 1508. Madonna and Child*

Fatima Ronquillo
p104: *Wounded Hand with Lover's Eye, 2012*

Sabrina Rowan Hamilton
p87: *Untitled, 2012*

Ursula Sternberg
p6: *Hattie, 1975*

Jethro Tanner
p82: *Untitled, 2009*

Thompson & Co
p12: *Bunty® © DC Thomson & Co. Ltd. 2014. Used By Kind Permission of DC Thomson & Co. Ltd*

Caragh Thuring
p49: *ACDC, 2008*

Tim & Sue
p102: *I Love Sex, 2002*

Caroline Walker
p20: *Transformation' by Caroline Walk. Oil on board, 2010*
p38 (right): *Display Case, 2010*
p110 (left): *Séance, 2013*

Mark Wallinger
p148: *Half-Brother, Exit to Nowhere © Mark Wallinger / Tate Images*

Francesca Woodman
p22: *Space Series, Rhode Island by Francesca Woodman © the Estate of Francesca Woodman*

PHOTOGRAPHY CREDITS

Harriet Anstruther
p10, p12 (third column top), p13 (top left), p16 (top left), p18 (top), p31 (right), p32, p34-35 (right), p56, p58, p62 (middle), p80, p81, p85, p95 (left), p96 (right), p98 (right, left), p99 (left), p101, p108, p110 (middle), p116, p120 (right), p121, p128 (left), p134 (right), p136, p141, p143, p149 (left), p154-155

Henry Bourne
p13 (second column, top), p14, p17, p19, p24, p26 (left), p28 (right), p24 (right), p26 (right), p29 (right), p30, p38 (left), p39, p42 (left), p48, p51 (left), p57, p64, p65, p70 (left), p79, p82 (left), p86 (middle, right), p100, p102, p103, p106-107, p117 (left), p131, p149 (right), p152

Henry Braham
p51 (right)

Dave Burdon
p98 (second from right)

Christopher Burke
p12 (second column, bottom)

ChinellatoPhoto
p106-107 *Courtesy of Getty Images*

Anton Corbijn
p117 (right) *Courtesy of Getty Images*

John Deakin
p135 (right) *Courtesy of Getty Images*

Robert Doisneau
p135 (left) *Courtesy of Getty Images*

James Ephraums
p158 *Courtesy of Getty Images*

Chris Felver
p119 (right)

James Fennel
p44-45, p47, p50, p58 (right), p59, p66-67, p71 (left), p88, p93, p97 (right), p126, p142, p150, p151

Enrique Gomez
p21 (right):

Henry Guttmann
p27 *Courtesy of Getty Images*

Dorling Kindersley
Cover *Courtesy of Getty Images*

Quintin Lake
p34 (left), p36-37, p40-41, p52 (left), p54 (right), p60, p63, p72, p74-75, p78 (left), p89 (right), p109 (right), p111, p122-123, p132

Andrew Lamb
p46, p71 (right), p84, p87

Richard Lewisohn
p43

James Merrell
p115

Santiago Moreno
p25, p33, p49, p52 (right), p53, p55, p68 (right), p70 (right), p73, p89 (left), p92, p114, p140

Michael Ochs
p146 (left)

Marcus Peel
p6, p12 (first column, bottom), p29 (left), p42 (right), p61, p67, p76, p77, (left), p83 (right), p86 (left), p95, p96 (left), p109 (left), p112, p113 (bottom right), p120 (left), p124, p127, p129, p134 (left), p144, p145

Harper Collins Publishers
p130 (right)

Jeremy Stigter
p12 (top)

Jethro Tanner
p82 (right)

Pia Tryde
p21 (left), p23, p26 (right), p68 (left), p91, p94, p96 (left), p97 (left), p137, p138-139

Christ Tubbs
p78 (right)

Baron Walmon
p12 (fourth column, bottom)

BIBLIOGRAPHY

The Way of All Flesh, Samuel Butler.
Grant Richards 1903.

Martin Chuzzlewit, Charles Dickens.
Chapman & Hall 1844.

Little Dorrit, Charles Dickens.
Bradbury and Evans, 1855 in monthly format and 1857 in book format.

On the Road, Jack Kerouac.
Viking Press, 1957.

The Architecture of Happiness, Alain de Botton
Vintage International (8 April 2008)

The Poetics of Space, Gaston Bachelard
Beacon Press; New Edition (1 Mar 1992)

No Man Is An Island, John Donne
London - The Folio Society (2004)

The Eyes of the Skin: Architecture & the Senses,
Juhani Pallasmaa
John Wiley & Sons; 2nd Edition (22 April 2005)

Miracles and Idolatry, Voltaire
Penguin (25 Aug 2005)

Housing Problems: Writing and Architecture in Goethe, Walpole, Freud, and Heidegger (Meridian: Crossing Aesthetics)
Stanford University Press (15 July 2008)

Signs of the Times: A Portrait of the Nation's Tastes,
Nicholas Barker & Martin Parr
Cornerhouse Publications; First Edition (3 Jan 1992)

The Secret Power of Beauty, John Armstrong
Penguin; New Edition (27 Jan 2005)

The Tropic of Cancer, Henry Miller
John Calder Ltd (1963)

*Three Chance Meetings Francis Bacon -
Lucien Freud - Diego Giacometti,* Anton Astbury
Mailer Press; 1st Edition (2010)

Elsie de Wolfe: The Birth of the Modern Interior,
Penny Sparke, Mitchell Owens
Acanthus Press, U.S. (5 Sep 2005)

On Altering Architecture, Fred Scott
Routledge; New Ed (13 Dec 2007)

Louise Bourgeois: Destruction of the Father/ Reconstruction of the Father: Writings and Interviews 1923 - 1997, Louise Bourgeois, Marie-Laure Bernadac, Hans-Ulrich Obrist
Violette Editions; New Edition (18 May 1998)

ACKNOWLEDGEMENTS

I'd like to thank Catharine Snow who generously commissioned me to write this book & edited it without flap. Prodigious thanks goes to graphic designer Dave Burdon who is quite simply, a white-hot genius. To Tom Dixon for his bounteous foreword. Appreciation also to Sam Kirkby who grappled effortlessly with multiple layout changes, & equally to Simonne Waud for her patience. Thanks also, to Jane Withers whose suggestions on the structure of the book, encouraged me to create something entirely personal. I am very grateful indeed to my wonderful staff at Harriet Anstruther Studio, for giving me the provision and time to finish the book, whilst working on multiple other studio projects.

Mostly however I would like to thank my family; my mother Susan who astounds me with her energy, drive & enthusiasm & whose fearlessness has driven me to push myself; my husband Henry Bourne whose beautiful photographs adorn these pages, & without whose big-heartedness & talent, there probably wouldn't be a book, and lastly to my remarkable daughter Celestia Nell, who inspires me like no other. Thank you all for your patience, love & support.